Piki Goes to College

Joan M. Hellquist

Author and Illustrator

Piki Goes to College

Hi there! My name is Piki. Piki rhymes with sneaky, which yes, I can be sneaky at times. But my forever friend and person, Joan, chose that name for me because of the color of my coat. It's sort of blue. Piki is the name of the bread that Hopi women make from ground blue corn. So I guess you could say that I have a Native American name. I'm very proud of that.

I met Joan when I thought I was in jail. But I wasn't really in jail. I was in an animal shelter. Animal Control found me wandering the streets of Rio Rancho, New Mexico. They caught me and brought me to the shelter in their truck. It was all pretty scary and then they put me in this cell, uh, kennel. I was in the second of a long line of indoor-outdoor kennels and when Joan saw me, she immediately stooped down to my level. She talked to me quietly and I could tell that she liked me. I liked her too. Joan wasn't afraid of me and she let me lick her fingers.

A couple of days later, the jail people took me to a veterinarian who examined me and gave me medicine that made me fall asleep. When I woke up, my stomach was sore where they had spayed and tattooed me. I was excited that I now had a tattoo, but not about being taken back to the shelter.

Later that afternoon Joan arrived and gave me my own new collar that had a tag with my name on one side and my address and phone number on the other side. Then she took me to my new forever home. I was happy to get out of jail and go home with Joan.

When we got to Joan's house, my new home, Joan introduced me to my siblings, two Jack Russell Terriers. My brother's name is Buster and my sister's name is Raleigh. Raleigh is the smallest of the three of us, but she let me know right away that she was the boss!

Joan has four neighbors but they don't live very close. There is a bumpy road from the main road down to our house. Behind the house is a pen with a brick floor and a metal roof where Buster and Raleigh stay part of the day. They told me that because they are little, they have to be either inside the house or in the outside pen with a roof so that coyotes and owls can't get to them. I'm not sure what coyotes or owls are, but they don't sound very friendly. At the side of the house is a fenced in area where I can run around. Raleigh and Buster can be out there with me as long as Joan is there with us.

There are a lot of rules at Joan's house! There are rules about where and when you eat, where you sleep, no begging, stay off of the furniture and pee and poop outside. Joan calls that last rule, house training. It seems to me more like, outside of the house training.

Joan started working with me on what Raleigh and Buster referred to as basic training. This includes learning words and what the words mean like come, sit, stay and down. When Joan started taking me on walks around the neighborhood, I was given a new piece of gear called a nose halter. It sort of looks like a muzzle, but it isn't a muzzle. I must admit it is not my favorite thing that she has given me. It doesn't hurt or anything like that, it just gives Joan more control, by keeping me beside her when we go for walks. She also said I'd need it when we started working together. I wondered if that meant we were getting a job.

Within a few months, I got the idea of all of these rules and commands, even the house training. Then Joan and I began going to Rick and Heather's house, which is not far from where Animal Control picked me up. Rick and Heather talked a lot to Joan and the other people who were there with their dogs. We all went out into their backyard where we learned how to behave when we were around other dogs and people. They taught us what to do when we were on our leashes and to listen to our person, come when called and even how to play nicely with the other dogs...no biting, mouthing, jumping on or tackling.

After a while, I figured out that both Joan and I were going to school together. She was learning how to be a teacher or instructor and how to train me. I was Joan's student and I was being trained to be a good dog, to behave myself, to listen carefully to her and to learn to do a lot of things. When we finished school, Joan would be an instructor and I would be a special dog. I didn't yet know if I'd have a title or not, but I hoped so.

Soon after the training began, Joan and I met either with Heather and her dog, Kita, or Rick with his dog, Jackson, at a hardware department store. That first day at the store, we met Rick and Jackson outside. Jackson and I were officially introduced. Then we all went inside and immediately turned to the right into a quiet aisle along the front of the building. I, well, I'm very embarrassed to say this, but I went a little crazy.

There were VERY TALL shelves on both sides of us, a lot of people around, a funny slippery floor and odd lighting. All of that made it a very scary place! Rick sat down on the floor with me and showed Joan a way to get me to calm down. Rick called it Steel and Cloth. He held me on the floor in front of him in a particular way so that when I'd squirm, he tightened his hold on me. That was the Steel part. When I'd relax and stay still, Rick loosened his hold and gently held me. That was the Cloth part.

As I got better at being in stores that allowed all dogs in them, Joan was beginning to train me to be able to go to stores with different challenges like narrower aisles, floors that reflected light, different smells, louder noises, all sorts of things.

To go to those other stores, I had to earn my vest. To earn my vest I had to listen to Joan and follow all of the rules well enough when we were in public, so that I could go into stores that didn't allow just any dog in them.

The vest seemed to mean that the dog wearing it was a very special dog. Kita and Jackson already had vests. Their vests were different colors and had zippered pockets and patches with writing on them. The vests made them look very important and really cool.

It took several more weeks, but I did it, I earned my vest! What I didn't know was that when I earned my vest, I also got a mat that matched my vest. The mat was for me to lie on when we went out to a restaurant or coffee shop. I learned that if we were out somewhere and Joan was sitting down, she'd put my mat on the floor by her feet and that was where I was supposed to lie down.

My vest and mat are both a bright teal blue color. The vest has pockets and some patches on it. I can't read so I don't know what the writing on the patches means but they look really official.

After I earned my vest and mat, the next kind of store we went to was a big sporting goods store. After we'd been to that store many times, I was tired of Joan asking me to do so many things. I was still pretty young then, the dog equivalent of a teenager. I decided to rebel right there on the slippery floor where two wide aisles crossed.

I plopped myself on the floor on my side and wouldn't get up. This was my signature move which became known as the Piki Flop and Roll. Joan went through several ways she'd been taught to get me to stand up, but I wouldn't budge. While Rick was making suggestions to Joan as to what to try next to get me up on my feet, Jackson just stared at me with a look of, "What do you think you are doing?" on his face. I could tell that he was very embarrassed that I was making a scene right there in the store.

Just before Joan was going to mop the floor with me, I did get up. She didn't seem very pleased with my performance that day.

There was another class that we had on Sundays. It was my least favorite class and I think because of my behavior, Joan's least favorite too.

There were some students with their dogs at this class that weren't in any of our other classes. I frequently demonstrated the Piki Flop and Roll for the other dogs there at the Sunday class, thinking that maybe they'd like to try it. But they seemed unimpressed. Then Joan began demonstrating the Steel and Cloth maneuver on me, showing the other dog parents what to do when their dog misbehaved.

Now I don't want you to get the idea that during this time that it was all work for Joan and me. I learned that when Joan put my vest and nose halter on me, we were going to go out in public and I was Piki, the special dog who had a job to do.

Once she took off my special gear, I was just Piki, the pet dog. Joan would take me out to the fenced in area beside the house and she would throw a ball for me. I guess I was supposed to pick it up and bring it back to her, but I never really got into that ball chasing activity. Sometimes I'd go in the fenced area with friends, like Sebastian, and we'd run around and play. It was lots of fun.

When I was inside the house, I started practicing my version of doggie yoga. I would lie down on my back and strike a pose that relaxes me and always makes Joan laugh. I don't understand why she still thinks it is funny. I think I look quite graceful doing my yoga.

Rick and Heather had been with us enough times to know that I didn't always behave. One day Rick said to Joan, "If you can train Piki to be a Service Dog, you can train any dog."

Hmmm, Service Dog, I wondered if that was what I was training to be? And did he mean I'd been difficult? Well, okay, maybe I had been difficult, sometimes.

Rick, Jackson, Joan and I were at a department store one day. I was behaving pretty well and of course, Jackson and I were wearing our vests and nose halters. A mom with her small child came near to us and the child said, "Mommy, doggies!"

The mom quietly said, "We must not bother them, those dogs are going to college."

I thought, "Wow, college, I'm going to college? That must be what you have to do to be a Service Dog."

Because I found out that I was going to college to be a Service Dog, I tried to ask Joan a lot of questions about them. She tried to explain the basics to me in words, but I couldn't understand them all. You see, we don't speak the same language. But here is what she told me. Maybe you'll understand her words.

To have a Service Dog, the person, who may be a child all the way up to a very old person, must have some kind of disability. The disability can be from an illness or disorder like epilepsy, hearing problems, arthritis or diabetes. Or they might have had an injury or other problems that made their body not work very well. Some of those include cerebral palsy, spina bifida, stroke, back injury or amputation. A Service Dog can also help with disabilities you can't see, like autism, traumatic brain injury or post-traumatic stress disorder.

To be a Service Dog, the dog must be trained to do specific tasks to help their person with their disability.

Service Dogs can go anywhere that the public can regularly go, like schools, stores, restaurants, medical offices, hospitals, buses, trains and airplanes.

Service Dogs cannot go to places where the public is not allowed. A few examples of those are the kitchens in restaurants, operating rooms in hospitals, clean rooms in factories or people's houses, unless the owner gives permission.

Little by little, as I got older, Joan and I had been out in many different public places together. I got better in those places and finally gave up the Piki Flop and Roll. I didn't really want to give it up, but.... Restaurants were the most difficult for me. I still don't quite understand why I have to lie down under the table, I can't check for dropped crumbs and I can't lie down in the aisle between tables. After all, there is a lot more room there where I can spread out and be more comfortable. But it isn't about my comfort, it is about being a well mannered dog, helping my person and not getting in anyone's way.

Many people think that Service Dogs are always big like German Shepherds, Labrador and Golden Retrievers or a doodle dog like a Labradoodle or a Goldendoodle. But if the person doesn't need their dog to do things that require a lot of strength or reaching high places, a smaller dog can be a Service Dog too. The dog shouldn't be so small, however, that they might get tripped over while in public.

I met my little friend Teddy at Rick and Heather's house. He was going through some training to be a Service Dog even though he is a lot smaller than I am. He always looks so handsome in his blue vest.

Most Service Dogs are trained by organizations that get their dogs when they are puppies, from a breeder. After basic training, often in private homes, they work with a specific trainer to learn about behaving at home and in public and how to perform many tasks to help their person. People with disabilities apply for a Service Dog from the organization and sometimes have to wait years to get theirs. This kind of training is very expensive, so most of these organizations depend on donations.

You may have heard about dogs that help the blind. They not only have to go to college, but they go to the equivalent of graduate school! Service Dogs for the blind get extremely specialized training and because of that, it can take longer to train them than other Service Dogs.

My training method was developed by Rick and Heather and allows the person with the disability or one of their family members to get their dog, usually from a shelter or sometimes from a breeder, if that's what they prefer. Their dog lives with their person and is trained by their person with the guidance and additional training from their Service Dog Instructor/Trainer like Joan. This method allows each of us to get to know our forever family right away and bond with our person during the training. This way too, we learn exactly the skills that we need to be able to perform to help our person.

In my case, once Joan is an Instructor/Trainer, I will go with her when she is doing her job. She teaches both the person and dog and the dog learns also by watching me as I learned by watching Jackson and Kita.

It took what seemed like forever, but both Joan and I finally graduated. We had completed the course together! There was a graduation ceremony for Joan and me and two other new Instructor/Trainers, Kirsten and Nathaniel Lukas, and their dogs.

That hat I'm wearing is called a mortarboard. When people graduate from high school or college, they always wear one of these along with a matching gown. I didn't get a gown.

Some Tasks Service Dogs Can Do to Help Their Person

Alerting their person that they are going to have a seizure

Staying with them before, during and after a seizure

Reminding a caregiver what to do when their person is having a seizure, such as getting oxygen

Going to get someone or a specific person to help

Alerting a diabetic that their blood sugar is too high or low

Alerting the hearing impaired to specific sounds or danger

Helping with balance while walking, helping to get out of a chair or up after a fall

Opening and closing doors, lights on and off

Fetching specific items, picking up things from the floor

Finding misplaced objects

Carrying items

Walking beside or pulling a wheelchair

Reminding their person that it is time to take medication

Being with their person if they are upset or in pain

Stepping between their person and others to lessen stress

Helping their person gain more independence at home and in public

Reassuring family or caregivers that someone else is looking after and helping their loved one at all times

Many other tasks can be taught depending on what the person with the disability needs for their individual help

I've told you several things about Service Dogs, so that if you are in a store and you see a Service Dog, you'll know we have had special training. You'll know that we help our person, who has some sort of disability, to perform tasks they have trouble doing or are unable to do for themselves.

As long as it's okay with the adult(s) you are with, you may want to let the person with the dog know what you've learned about Service Dogs.

Here is what you SHOULDN'T do if you see a person with a Service Dog

Don't pet the dog. The dog is working and shouldn't be distracted. Only pet the dog if the person specifically gives you permission to do so.

Don't ask the dog's name. Hearing their name is also distracting for the dog.

Don't make loud sounds or sudden movements. Both of these actions can distract and/or scare the dog.

Don't ask the Service Dog's person about their disability or what their dog does to help them. This is very private information and the person only shares this information with someone who has a personal, family, medical or professional role in their life.

So, bye for now. Maybe I'll see you at a store or restaurant
sometime. But until then, thanks for listening to my story.

                    Your friend,
                    Piki, S.D.
                         Service Dog

                    (I have a title now!)

In Loving Memory of

Raleigh

I miss them both a lot.

Buster

In Honor of My New Brothers

Teddy

Sebastian aka
The Handsome Dude

p.s. Whenever Joan and I go out in public, people ask what breed I am. They usually guess that I'm an Australian Shepherd, but I'm not. I had my DNA done and I'm part Border Collie and part Plott Hound. The Plott Hound is the state dog of North Carolina. Joan used to live there.

I'm not a doodle dog or other named designer breed. Joan calls me a Border Plott. So I'm my own designer breed!

Joan M. Hellquist
Author and Illustrator

Joan M. Hellquist has been an animal lover and artist all of her life. She grew up in Summit, NJ, but Placitas, NM has been home since 1988. The New Mexico high desert light, landscape and wildlife continues to nurture her soul.

Joan worked in healthcare and continues to do her artwork, from pastel portraits and landscapes to wildlife images painted on Native American made hand drums. In 2015 she became a Service Dog Instructor/Trainer and since 2017 has volunteered as a Bereavement Facilitator at the NM Children's Grief Center. Joan and her dogs, Piki and Teddy, share their home with Joan's friend, Deb, and Deb's dog, Sebastian.

Information for Mom, Dad and Other Adults

IF YOU OWN A BUSINESS you need to know what the rules are and pass that information on to your employees.

Service Dogs must be allowed into areas of the business that all people are allowed to enter.

Business owners and employees may only ask the person with the Service Dog two questions.

Do you have a disability?
The person with the Service Dog only needs to answer yes. The person does not have to say nor can they be forced to say exactly what their disability is. Some are obvious and some don't show at all. The only people without disabilities who may have a Service Dog with them are caregivers or Instructor/Trainers.

What does the dog do to help you with your disability?
This pertains to what tasks the dog does to help the person with their disability. "She lets me know when my blood sugar is too high or low." "He helps me keep my balance." The person with the Service Dog is not required to demonstrate these tasks upon request or demand.

Online Information

www.ada.gov "Search ADA" will be in the upper right of the opening page.   Enter "Service Animals." This will provide detailed information about Service Dogs and the law.

www.petsandhelpingdogs.com Information on Service Dog training, the ADA, behavioral rehabilitation. Nathaniel Lukas trained with Rick and Heather Dillender.

www.ralphcleverworkingdogsrehabilitation.com Information on Service Dogs and other working dog training, behavioral rehabilitation and socialization. Kirsten trained with Rick and Heather Dillender.

Books about Piki's Training

Dillender, Rick, and Heather Dillender. *From Shelter to Service Dog: A Practical Guide to Behavioral Rehabilitation.* 2013.

Dillender, Rick, and Heather Dillender. Redekopp, Nathaniel Lukas, Editor. *PTSD and Service Dogs: A Training Guide for Sufferers.* 2014.

Unfortunately Rick and Heather Dillender's business, A Fresh Perspective Dog Training, is no longer active. Rick and Heather have moved on to other pursuits in their lives. Please see their two books, or contact either of the two websites above if you'd like further information.

All Adults Please Note!

If you see "Official Service Dog IDs or Certificates" for sale online, there is nothing official about them. Organizations that train Service Dogs or individual trainers may provide an ID indicating that the dog has been properly trained and by whom. But the Americans with Disabilities Act does not legally require certification from any organization or individual, as long as the dog is capable of performing at Service Dog ADA standards.

Unfortunately people continue to try to pass their pet off as a trained Service Dog. A vest, patch, ID or certificate does not prove that the dog is properly trained.

Pretending a dog is a Service Dog, when they aren't, hurts the legitimate Service Dog community by putting their access rights in jeopardy when untrained dogs show unsafe or disruptive behavior in public places.

This practice is dishonest, disrespectful and in some cases illegal.